GW01312925
GW 2275

BROUGH SUPERIOR SS100

Colin Simms

CONTENTS

ISBN 0 85429 364 7

A FOULIS Motorcycling Book

First published 1984

Published by:
Haynes Publishing Group
Sparkford, Yeovil,
Somerset BA22 7JJ

Distributed in USA by:
Haynes Publications Inc.
861 Lawrence Drive, Newbury
Park, California 91320, USA

Cover design: Rowland Smith
Page Layout: Mike King
Photographs: Andrew Morland
Road tests: The Motor Cycle and
Motor Cycling, courtesy of *EMAP*
Printed in England by: J.H. Haynes
& Co. Ltd

Titles in the *Super Profile* series

Ariel Square Four (F388)
BMW R69 & R69/S (F387)
BSA A7 & A10 Twins (F446)
BSA Bantam (F333)
Honda CB750 sohc (F351)
MV Agusta America (F334)
Norton Commando (F335)
Sunbeam S7 & S8 (F363)
Triumph Thunderbird (F353)
Triumph Trident (F352)
KSS Velocette (F444)

AC/Ford/Shelby Cobra (F381)
Austin-Healey 'Frogeye' Sprite (F343)
Corvette Stingray 1963-1967 (F432)
Ferrari 250GTO (F308)
Fiat X1/9 (F341)
Ford Cortina 1600E (F310)
Ford GT40 (F332)
Jaguar E-Type (F370)
Jaguar D-Type & XKSS (F371)
Jaguar Mk 2 Saloons (F307)
Jaguar SS90 & SS100 (F372)
Lancia Stratos (F340)
Lotus Elan (F330)
Lotus Seven (F385)
MGB (F305)
MG Midget & Austin-Healey Sprite (except 'Frogeye') (F344)
Morris Minor Series MM (F412)
Morris Minor & 1000 (ohv) (F331)
Porsche 911 Carrera (F311)
Rolls-Royce Corniche (F411)
Triumph Stag (F342)

B29 Superfortress (F339)
Boeing 707 (F356)
Harrier (F357)
Mosquito (F422)
Phantom II (F376)
P51 Mustang (F423)
Sea King (F377)
Super Etendard (F378)
Tiger Moth (F421)
Vulcan (F436)

Great Western Kings (F426)
Intercity 125 (F428)
V2 'Green Arrow' Class (F427)

Further titles in this series will be published at regular intervals. For information on new titles please contact your bookseller or write to the publisher.

FOREWORD

Much has already been written about the marque of Brough Superior, adding to the aura and the 'cloud of unknowing' around name and machine since the early 'twenties, and the realised dream of a man who can not be separated from his creation. In the Brough Superior cult, George Brough is the originator, author, designer, manufacturer, rider, master. George Brough demanded perfection with high performance, and his masterpiece is the SS 100, variants of which model (and no two are precisely alike) were long his personal steeds as they were also for other discriminating and demanding riders, Lawrence of Arabia amongst them. The long-distance trial and racing men found the SS 100 their best basis too, as some still do! Scarce and costly as all ideals must be, Brough Superior production ceased in 1940. Since 1924 only about 384 SS 100 had been built, and many survive today, and more than survive; a measure of their excellence and of their esteem. Like the other Brough Superior models, they made a substantial contribution to improvements in practical motorcycling since the first world war, and many of the features we now take for granted were pioneered by George Brough and his team, as the result of painstaking development and testing to the limits. The recent reversion to the vee-twin concept is remarkable, though no modern versions combine the quietness, fine finish, grace, high performance with docility, line pedigree of tried refinement, made-to-measure individuality and likely longevity of the Brough Superior SS 100.

In nearly twenty years of riding and owning Brough Superior machines, I have never yet been an SS 100 owner, but each SS 100 I **have** ridden has presented a different character of the manufacturer and of the owners, whose pride in their mounts and idealism for the '100' keeps these machines clear of massive modification. It is difficult to generalise from such individual machines; but I am much indebted to those owned by Ken Middleditch and John Weekly who have made their machines available for photography, and to other members of the friendly Brough Superior Club, which caters for men and women, and not necessarily owners. Much of this book derives from fellowship with some of these owners and former owners; chief amongst them the historian of the marque, Ronald Clark, whose *Brough Superior – The Rolls-Royce of Motorcycles* surely requires a further edition and is the standard work anyone must first acknowledge. Numerous other authors on the marque, not all in agreement any more than on any other emotive historical subject, have contributed to the information and the aura from which this introduction to a great motorcycle is some little distillation. Look at the photograph gallery. It was a very **beautiful** motorcycle, and remains so, and beauty of line with simplicity of components makes for much more than just 'fitness for purpose'!

Most of this book could not have been compiled without the co-operation of motorcycling periodicals, and it is indebted to years of the B.S. Club *Newsletter.* I have been lucky to have recorded conversations, some of them years ago, with long-term users of the marque; men who were and are themselves critical engineers and riders, and well able to express their idiosyncratic views. The Brough has always attracted such men. There is always a danger that the wish to be associated with some literary or historical figure, or a machine once pre-eminent in racing or sheer quality by possessing an SS 100, all these and more, will prove sufficient reason to own one of these motorcycles. Perhaps in a museum environment. Let us remember instead what most of those great figures, and the originator George Brough himself, would have said and what the machine says by its line and history, adaptability and liveliness itself. Ride, cherish, ride, revere. But ride!

To many such Brough Superior men, but perhaps especially Bill Gibbard, Ronald Clark, Peter Robinson and Peter Anderson, I say many thanks for my introduction!

Mention Brough Superior amongst motorcyclists, enlightened historians of the twentieth century, airmen, poets, Rolls-Royce men, and any of these varied groups are likely to include connoisseurs who respect the name and can say something of it. For a marque in such limited production – more or less 3000 machines over some 20 years or so between the wars, a remarkable proportion have survived. Of these some hundreds only were the series of ohv sportsters and sports touring machines designated 'SS 100'. All were guaranteed a speed potential of 100 mph – in the early twenties, remember, when beaded edge tyres, belt rim brakes and bicycle frames abounded; George Brough was to change all that! But speed and handling, strength and reliability, aren't the only watchwords for which this expressive, expansive of horizons, machine has been known. Sheer quality of finish, sheer style and line and perhaps above all a real practical simplicity generally, characterize it. Jeff Clew's idea, this work has been patiently encouraged along by him and by Ronald Clark, but all errors and omissions are the fault of the author.

Notes on Bill Gibbard's *'Maintaining Your Brough Superior'* are taken from the author's review in *Motorcycle Sport,* May 1981, with thanks to that excellent journal's editor, Cyril Ayton.

Various owners and former owners have discussed their machines and allowed them to be inspected, ridden or compared, especially Ken Middleditch and John Weekly whose machines have formed the basis for the photographic gallery here. Further acknowledgement is also due to Aenne Weber and Margaret Wilson, who have patiently typed and retyped manuscripts of varying legibility.

Colin Simms

HISTORY

The origins of the SS 100 are deep in the desire of one man to produce the machine he wanted, which would do better than any contemporary design the strenuous and adventurous tasks of speed and endurance, stamina and flexibility, versatility and reliability he required of it. From proprietary parts built onto and around his own frames, tanks, mudguards, exhaust systems, pannier fittings and of course the Harley-Davidson-type Castle forks with his own clean handlebar design brazed-on. Parts that proved fallible in use were sent back to manufacturers, whilst some components were specially designed or redesigned better and stronger when found wanting. The Brough Superior feedback proved valuable; Sturmey Archer and Norton gearboxes benefited, as well as Enfield wheels, JAP and, later, AMC big-twin engines when JAP were eventually unwilling to keep up with the rider-manufacturer's demands for improvements. J.A. Prestwich had been prepared to build special engines for George Brough from the start, such was the prestige his sporting successes and his luxury-mount ambitions commanded. 'Special for Brough' had been JAP designs since the advanced and high-performance '90 Bore' ohv of 1920 which powered his 'Mark I', in many ways the precursor of the first 'SS 100'. To house the redesigned 85.7 x 85mm ohv engine, a cradle frame designed with H.Le Vack replaced the earlier diamond for the Olympia Show of 1924, when the '100 was launched, as the 1925 catalogue declared, 'with a guarantee signed by the Maker, that the machine has actually been timed over 100 mph for a quarter of a mile', and, as the 1926 catalogue reported, 'hands off' stability at 95 mph. Such performance, at a time when 60 or 70 mph was considered remarkable enough in a production machine, set, and continued to set, new standards which attracted a distinct and distinguished market for the marque. Nothing stood still, laurels were never rested on. For the 1926 Olympia Show the 'Alpine Grand Sports' version of the SS 100 was ready, powered by the new 80 x 99 mm JAP, with a four-gallon petrol tank and tailored rigid panniers, intended for fast long-distance touring. For the racing man there was soon the 'Pendine' version, named after speed successes at Pendine Sands by the SS 100; this had a higher compression engine, 'one pair of foot rests placed high up and well back', narrow mudguards, close ratio gears and a guarantee that the machine had exceeded 110 mph before dispatch.

In 1928 the Alpine Grand Sports was priced £165; but there was available from 1927 for about £100 the overhead 680; George Brough's 'Miniature SS 100', and ultimately a 500 ohv, and 680cc, 750cc and 1096cc sidevalves alongside the long-running SS 80 1000cc s.v. The flagship, or as one journalist put it, the 'battle cruiser' of the line, was always the SS 100. Even the very limited-production fours of 1927 and '28, and the plans for the Dream flat four later, were not to replace the '100 as the marque leader from even this ingenious maker.

Amongst the fitments pioneered and developed, some in regular usage then, and none for cosmetic effect originally, were flyscreens, twin headlamps, dipping headlamps, finger adjusters on cables, crashbars, legshields, prop stands, pannier cases and hinged rear mudguards. And, of course, if you so desired, you could have an SS 100 supplied fitted with a sidecar. George Formby had one of these for many years, and **used** it. It was one of the last SS 100s, 1939, and he had it until his death in 1961. I have an Alpine Grand Sports sidecar, made at George Brough's Nottingham works to the latest and best Austrian (Felber) and British (George Brough) patents, far ahead of its time.

The history of the SS 100, and of the Brough Superior in general, was as bound up with its competition successes as any other marque with great potential, and in this case the links between works personalities and racers, the feedback into production models from racing, and above all at the beginning the achievements of George Brough and the production and publicity gains he made of them, are close and legendary and in a brief survey we can only be very selective and partial. Spurred by George Brough, J.A. Prestwich's had, after two years' experiment to beat the Americans to the most efficient big vee-twin, produced their 50° 85.7 x 85mm, KTOR racing 8/45 motor, the basis of the early SS 100 and generally preferred to the 1928-33 80 x 99 mm JTOR 8/50, for its rather better bottom-end torque. Late in 1933 the SS 100 became powered by a development of the 8/50 engine, the 8/75, capable of 74 bhp, but George Brough soon favoured the 'square' AMC (85.5 x 85.5 mm) with either 7 or 8 to I compression ratio, and this was the final engine fitted to the Brough Superior SS 100 from late 1935 until the end of production about the beginning of the second world war.

Such power takes some controlling on English roads, in competition or in touring, despite smooth power delivery! So it is not surprising to find a front wheel brake appearing on the modified Harley-Davidson forks where American highways, habits and lack of similar competition hadn't dictated one. Steering equally good, solo or sidecar, at speed, with no modification necessary to steering geometry, the same machine could be used solo or sidecar in subsequent races, the massive head lug casting providing rigidity where so many competitors broke their down-tube. The three-stay rear subframe gave rigidity of chain line and back end, which you'll also see on the Norton cradle frame just a little later. Just one feature. A short list of some successes will help put matters in perspective.

Before the appearance of the SS 100, the years 1921-3 saw more than 50 wins in British and Irish major events; some trials like the 'Land's End', the 'Edinburgh', the 'Manville Trophy', the 'Colmore Cup', the 'Scottish Six Days'; some Speed Trials like the 'Brighton', and the 'East Midland ACU'; some sprints as at Pendine; some hill climbs at Nuneaton, Newport, Bournemouth, Croydon, Bristol, Rochester, Bradford and Stalybridge; races run by the B.M.C.R.C. (Bemsee) and the Leinster (the '100' and the '50'), the Ulster and, of course, Brooklands track where H. Le Vack (who helped develop the SS 100) was already in charge of seven World's Records when the SS 100 was being evolved. At Arpajon he, and then Freddie Dixon (130 mph for the kilometre, 1927) and then Le Vack again in 1929 and 1930, claimed the World's best for the flying kilometre (129.06) and the flying mile (128.23), after George Brough himself at Arpajon in 1928 made the World's fastest one-way kilometre at 130.6 mph.

George Brough's achievements alone would fill a book such as this, but we must not forget his staff at the Brough Superior Works; Harold 'Oily' Karslake's early Golds in long-distance trials (perhaps not surprisingly, he was the originator of the prop-stand!); Ronald Storey's racing successes from 1927 including penetrating between the uprights of Saltburn pier with George Brough in 1928 at over 122 mph, winning a Pendine sprint, and 81.08 mph (ftd) over a standing half-mile at Brighton in 1932, beating all the cars into the bargain. What a likely lad to have as works tester!

Other great names included Jack Watson-Bourne, Jack Montgomery, Tommy Spann, Archduke Wilhelm of Habsburg (Austrian G.P. 100 kilometre race, 1924), Rudolf Arndt (Avus, Berlin 1926), Eddie Meyer the Brough Superior agent for Austria, E.C.E. Baragwanath, C.M. Needham, Jack Carr (too modest to talk of his successes to me shortly before he died but an almost unsung Brough Superior exponent from 1927 to 1934, when Noel Pope's and Eric Fernihough's names became regular) and from 1926, Bob Berry and then M.N. Mavrogordato. Their highlights include Fernihough's 143.39 mph for the kilometre at Brooklands in 1938, and Noel Pope's 124.51 mph lap at Brooklands in 1939, which stands for all time as the famous track has not opened post-war. The previous year he had set the Brooklands sidecar lap (AMC SS 100) at 106.6 mph, again for perpetuity!

Nor must we forget the vintage racing scene today and how competitive the '100 remains, even amongst modern machinery. From J.O. Cunliffe's (1926 SS 100) exploits in the early sixties through, for example, R.B. Knight's racer based on 27/30 models, to Dr. Beyer's (1929 Alpine Grand Sports) first at the Nürburgring in 1981, runs the continuing tradition and thread of excellence of the SS 100.

EVOLUTION

It is about 44 years since the last SS 100 rolled out of the 'Brufsup' works in Nottingham; a big machine from a small works! In the twenty-one years of Brough Superior production, the concept and the reality of this high-performance, high quality, highly efficient, highly finished, highly honoured, highly reliable and highly sought-after production machine had been evolved; a true 'super-bike' indeed.

In living things, the origination of new species from old ones over many generations from the stress of changing conditions and demands, a concept we owe largely to Darwin, may be thought remote from the world of motorcycles! Yet the idea of development of fitness to place, circumstances and requirements is essential. The 'evolution' of a manufactured thing, implying production over a considerable length of time, involves an 'opening-out' of its maker's mind and of its own inner nature; a 'rolling out' of potential. This notion of development under market forces is no less useful in the understanding of a marque than is that of natural selection in the origin of species from species.

Every time we buy a motorcycle, in a greater or lesser degree according to its production-runs, it affects the manufacturer, his suppliers, the trade, and of course our own taste and use: even sales data represent some feed-back. How much influence this had on the development of the early Brough Superior models, when almost every first owner, even from the police batches, had his detailed preferences, and often also suggestions made to him at the works, built into the specification, is open to speculation. The works records cards for most machines to the point of dispatch are available, and without them it would be impossible to even approach the original when restoring or rebuilding. So many individual machines were or are modified to different owners' tastes and requirements that there is no such thing as a standard or uniform SS 100, or any other Brough Superior for that matter. Nevertheless the history of the factory production of this model can be, thanks to records, rarity and respect, pieced together.

In this process past and present owners, especially the late P.J.C.Robinson and W.Gibbard, and Ronald Clark and others happily still with us, as well as a host of other contributors to the Brough Superior *Newsletter, Quarterly Journal,* other motorcyling periodicals, and correspondence, must be acknowledged.

'The SS 100', George Brough wrote in his catalogue of 1926 models, 'is a machine made essentially for an experienced MotorCyclist who realises that just as a racehorse needs more attention than a hunter so does a SS 100, with its colossal output of power, require more attention than the average sports machine. Give it the necessary attention and you have a machine that can always be relied upon to show its back number plate to anything on wheels likely to be met with on the roads.' Such, incidentally, is an example of the sales prose of the manufacturer; not out of date today and from a time when good English was invariably written about motorcycles. Back to 1925, and let us stay for a moment with the B.S. catalogue. An illustration shows the SS 100 'hands off' at an estimated speed of 95 mph. There follow pages of illustrated examples of successes in 1925, and of eulogies from owners and press comments, including this from 'Ixion'; 'Everybody is copying his pull-up handle, and no doubt in due course everybody will copy his prop-stand' and from 'Clarion'; 'the SS 100 Brough Superior is the most magnificent motorcycle ever produced, and it does credit to its rider-manufacturer.' But none of this gives us specifications, and anatomy is vital in evolution.

The early SS 100 had the 85.7 x 85mm, KTOR JAP engine, its tulip valves later being replaced by owners with the 'Dirt' type that has circlip collets, as JAP made spares for their Dirt engines which were widely available during the early thirties; I once in an emergency found a set in a cycle shop in a remote country market village! The SS 100 also had 37lb steel flywheels of nine inches diameter. The gearbox was the Sturmey-Archer Extra H.W.(heavyweight) or 'Special Brough'. The steering head was so strong, almost box section and reassuringly braced the single down tube which divided to cradle the engine and gearbox on its eloquent way to the rear wheel via three stays, the middle one housing the four-stud gearbox on a platform integral with a hefty lug brazed round the seat pillar tube. In case you are getting the impression that this is going to be a heavy machine, the all-up weight would prove not a lot over 320lbs, depending on equipment, decidedly less than even the sporting middleweights of today!

The Harley-Davidson fork had so impressed George Brough that he had copies made, with trifling variations on Harley-Davidson features, provisionally protected by British Patent 3941 (January

1925, George Brough and H.Karslake) but apparently never confirmed! They were made in his works as the 'Castle' fork and marketed by the Castle Fork and Accessory Company. These forks were the basis of the Brough Superior's handling so very well, with a very puny front brake at first, although eventually an eight-inch brake would be available; it is usual to hear complaints about the braking of the early models but they were better than many or most at their time. It proved difficult to design and fit an adequate brake to the Harley-Davidson type of parallel-ruler fork, but in due course a good one was evolved. The sense of balance, on a motorcycle, obviously depends in the eyes as well as the semicircular canals of the inner ear! The twin top tubes protruding above the steering-head of the Brough Superior fitted with a Castle fork provide points or parallels of reference very reassuring, very interesting to ride behind. Girder-type forks give very little variation in wheelbase, avoid the sinking feeling on braking so common otherwise, and provide rigidity with lightness such that one wonders whether the universal 'teles' of today are necessarily superior.

Evolution implies an increase in complexity, and for the practical motorcyclist this can be a chilling idea, associated with unnecessary fiddly-bits and additions which might hardly gild the lily. Forks are not the only component to have become very complicated. The Bentley and Draper spring frame, available at extra cost, was an early swinging arm system, not very robust but an aid in high speed roadholding.

All Brough engines required a forked connecting rod and a blade rod running inside it, using the same crankpin bearing and avoiding the slight rocking couple side-by-side conrods give to other designs more familiar today. That was an **avoidance** of complexity. There is some evidence that George Brough himself realised that his masterpiece had become a little too civilised towards the end of its production run, a little less rorty and a little more complex than he had intended, and he himself began to consider his 60° vee-engined 1150 JAP his favourite. For some people, myself and Peter Robinson amongst them, 'George could have put his pencil and paper away in 1925', to quote P.J.C.R.

And to quote favourite lines of George Brough's from Kipling's *'The Mary Gloster'*:

They have copied all they could follow,
but they couldn't copy my mind,
And I left 'em sweating and stealing
a year and a half behind.

(More, surely, than that short time ahead, though that was all he claimed in his catalogue.)

The evolution of the SS 100, its detail development as perhaps the greatest British superbike, relies for its greatest factor on the working-out of the conscious, and subconscious, ideas and ideals of George Brough, the Maker.

Some Brough Superiorities

1921 Pendine, $2\frac{1}{2}$ mile sprint. First (Handel-Davies). Land's End and Edinburgh Trials. Gold Medals (H. ('Oily') Karslake). Scottish Six Days Trial. Gold Medals (G. Brough, H. Karslake).

1922 ACU Six Days Trial. Gold Medal (J. Watson-Bourne). Land's End Trial. Gold Medal (J.D. Marvin).

1923 Brooklands, 200 miles solo. First (H. Le Vack), and 200 miles sidecar also: – setting seven World's Records in the process.

1924 Pendine, Welsh Tourist Trophy. First (C.M. Needham, SS 100). Baden-Baden Grand-Prix of Austria 100 kilometre. First (Archduke von Habsburg, SS 100).

1925 Southport. Standing mile, Flying kilometre, 50 miles and fastest motorcycle versus fastest car, all won by C.M. Needham, SS 100. Wiener Neustadt (Austria), Flying km. First (G. Brough, SS 100).

1926 Berlin (Avus). First (R. Arndt, SS 100). Pendine, Welsh TT. First (T. Spann, SS 100). Lago Percolilli. One Mile and 5 miles, standing start and flying start, all H. Baker (SS 100).

1927 St Andrews (Fife). 20 miles. First (R.J. Braid, SS 100). Saltburn Sands ftd. A. Greenwood, SS 100. Salzburg Grand-Prix. First (E. Meyer, SS 100).

1928 Doncaster, unlimited; G. Brough (sidecar), L. Currie (solo). Saltburn, kilometre. First, R.W. Storey 122.09 mph; Second, G. Brough 121.9 mph. Arpajon, kilometre (one-way) World's Fastest Solo, 130.6 mph.

1929 Budapest, solo. First, E. Meyer 115 mph (sidecar, first, E. Meyer 95 mph). Arpajon (two-ways) H. Le Vack, 129.05 mph. World's fastest solo.

1930 Arpajon, Flying kilometre. H. Le Vack 129.06 mph World's fastest solo. Flying mile, H. Le Vack 128.23 mph. Ingolstadt (Bavaria) E. Meyer, sidecar record 113.98 mph.

1931 Pendine, Welsh TT, 50 mile race and 100 mile race, J.H. Carr, SS 100. Gatwick, Sprint $\frac{1}{4}$ mile solo, C.R. Hobbs 66.18 mph and sidecar 59.21 mph.

1932 Southport kilometre, J.H. Carr 110.7 mph, SS 100. Brighton $\frac{1}{2}$m ftd, R.W. Storey (beating all cars). $\frac{1}{2}$m ftd, E.C.E. Baragwanath (sidecar).

1934 Brighton. N.B. Pope 80.36 mph fastest solo (supercharged)

1935 Sellick's Beach (Australia) 5 miles G. Marques, SS 100
10 miles G. Marques, SS 100.
Donington, sidecar race (10 laps) K. Collett first 57.27 mph.

1936 Gatwick, E.C. Fernihough, 78 mph.
Brighton, E.C. Fernihough 90.0 mph. (course record).

1939 Brooklands, N.B. Pope. Lap record of 124.51 mph remains for all time, as this track closed shortly before the war.

And the Brough Superior SS 100 is still winning events; as witnessed Dr. J. Beyer's efforts in Germany ...

SPECIFICATION

SS 100 – summary of main specifications

1925	Harley/Castle front forks, Webb 5 inch front, right heel-operated rear brake
1926	Binks or Wex carb., Narrow $2\frac{1}{2}$ gallon petrol tank, integral oil tank, manual oilpump, KTOR JAP motor, Sturmey-Archer 3-speed heavyweight gearbox (direct lever), 21 inch wheels, throttle lever.
1927	as above except Enfield 8 inch front brake, toe operated rear brake, two float chamber carburettor, 3 gallon petrol tank, separate oil tank, tank lever gearchange, throttle lever or AMAC internal twistgrip.
1927	Pendine had Binks 'mousetrap' carburettor, dry sump JAP motor with Pilgrim pump, special for Brough (S.B.) gearbox, 19 inch rear wheel, rearset footrests.
1928 1929	Spring frame optional, JTO or JTOR JAP motor, tank lever or gearbox-mounted gear lever, throttle lever or AMAC external twistgrip.
1930	7 inch Enfield front brake JTO motor, tank lever gearchange, 19 inch wheels, Amal internal twistgrip throttle.
1930	Alpine Grand Sports JTOR JAP motor, tank top switch and thin headlamps.
1931 and 1932	no *significant* change; all Brough Superiors showed detail variations!
1933	Left toe operated rear brake, $3\frac{1}{2}$ gallon petrol tank, JTOR JAP motor, Amal internal twistgrip throttle and internal horn and headlamp wiring
1934	4 gallon petrol tank, duplex oil pumps, JTOS JAP motor, foot-change pivots on kickstart shaft, 4 inch x 19 inch tyres.
1935	$3\frac{1}{2}$ gallon petrol tank, AMC dry sump X2 motor and oil pump, footchange lever, 3.50 inch x 19 inch tyres.

1936 on	Norton gearbox; four-speed footchange.

NOTE: All carburettors after 1929 are of Amal manufacture. All rear brakes are of Enfield manufacture.

Probable production numbers: SS 100 and its derivatives, JAP motors, 281
SS 100 and its derivatives, AMC motors, 102 or 103
total c. 384.

The JAP engines

The 8.45 engine (85.7 x 85mm) was used from 1924. It had open rockers and pushrods, but enclosed return springs and tappets. The valves and the 6 springs may be replaced by 'dirt track' JAP components and a surprising number of JAP parts can be adapted from other JAP engines. Friendly relations with the Morgan club helps! The magneto was mounted ahead of the engine and driven by an enclosed chain. The Pendine version used a bevel-driven magneto, and both exhaust-pipes were along the offside. In 1928 the 8/50 80 x 99mm engine (JTO or JTOR), was similar to the KTOR except for enclosed pushrods, enclosed rockers, and lighter flywheels. In 1934 the 8/75 twin-camshaft, twin magneto, twin carburettor engine appeared, with dry sump lubrication (four oil pumps plus the separate spitting system for the rockers!).

Even the earliest frames, had very very rigid steering-heads. The frames bear a striking resemblance to the shorter, three-stay cradle frame used by Norton for their sporting CSI and ES2 models, and there was well-known collaboration between Brough and Norton on gearboxes once the Sturmey-Archer pattern had shown itself unfit for the big power output the later Brough Superior engines developed.

The Club holds record cards for 101 AMC-engined machines but there are 6 cards missing so probably 107 were built and perhaps a further few (as many as seven?) during and after the war from spares in stock. The latest known engine number in an SS 100 of this type is 1111; engines otherwise outside the sequence 1000-1106 are replacements. The proprietary AMC engine was, of course, fitted to other makes, including the Morgan car. Sixty of these SS 100 were rigid framed, 7 with the Bentley and Draper swinging arm, and thirty four using Brough's plunger frame, another 'first' for the little company. Detail specifications, of course, varied for the user, but most machines made before 1938 had Lucas MOV or MOVH Magdynos, and later ones the Lucas L2. A few had single-float carburettors, a few oversize or otherwise special tanks (T.E.Lawrence's tank, transferred from machine to machine, was of stainless steel) but nearly all had the same sprocket ratios of engine 23T, clutch 42T and rear 41T, representing high gears overall. Other 'standard' features tended to include pannier bags, Enfield hubs with John Bull rims, (26x3.50in and 27x400in Dunlop Fort tyres), Altette horns and Lycett pan saddles. Interestingly, when you look at 'superbikes' today, only one was dispatched with a rev-counter! Even of such a small number, laughable by (say) Japanese standards, many went abroad; to Argentina, Australia, Canada, Cuba, Poland, Sweden, the USA and other places. Seven were specially adapted for supply to Sheffield City Police.

The SS80/100 combined some of the features of both models in the early days, as if George Brough hadn't quite made up his mind. As something over twenty were made, and the rate of destruction of Brough Superiors is so low, a word on them seems appropriate, even though they had side valve motors. T.E. Lawrence was an early customer; and the first, unofficial, one was probably dispatched on 6th September, 1924. They had Harley-Davidson forks, before the improved Castle forks were available, and from May or June 1925 and until September 1926 at least, 'official' (works-designated) SS80/100s were as high-prestige bicycles as the SS100s. The motor, a JAP KTOR (or 8/35) or KTCY as available, was very carefully assembled. Late in 1927, Castles were beginning to be fitted to SS80s and the lines 'side valve' and 'overhead valve' had diverged more distinctly; the 100 was the top performance machine, produced as the 80/100s had been, to customers' specification.

More about the engines

8/45 KTOR (85.7 x 85mm)	Nov. 1924 – Nov. 1927 (open push rods and rocker-ends)
8/50 JTOR (80 x 99mm)	Nov. 1927 – Nov. 1930 (enclosed push rods and rocker-ends)
8/55 JTO(R) (80 x 99mm)	Nov. 1930 – 1933
8/75 JTOS (80 x 99mm)	announced 1933, probably not available until 1934
(BS)x2 (AJS)	announced 1935, probably not available until 1936

The AMC engines were of the AJS type, because of the flats on the rear cylinder finning where the rearward magneto of the AJS was fitted; invariably these engines have been referred to as 'Matchless', which is incorrect.

DECEMBER 11th, 1924.

The o.h.v. SS-100 BROUGH SUPERIOR.

IT is a somewhat difficult task to report on the road behaviour of the SS-100 Brough Superior.

There are few bases of comparison, and, while it would be easy, and truthful, to say that it is a very wonderful machine, that does not convey much to the type of man who is likely to buy one. The problem is increased by December weather providing far from ideal conditions for trying a solo motor cycle right at the top of the super-sports class.

Two things saved the situation in the case of the present writer. In the first place he has had considerable experience of earlier Brough Superiors, and owns a 1924 SS-80 with Webb forks; and, secondly, the weather factor did not prove so important as had been feared.

Expectations which are Unfulfilled.

Previously, the Webb-equipped SS-80 had been his ideal, and however much the new o.h.v. machine excited admiration, it was considered that nothing else could be so pleasant to handle on the road as the earlier model, which was a paragon of all a fast solo machine should be in road-holding, absence of wobble, and the general preservation of the rider's mental and physical comfort, under all sorts of conditions. The newcomer might be more suitable for its 100 m.p.h.—the other did not aspire to reach that pace—but it would certainly be less comfortable, less tractable, and less safe in ordinary use.

The first mile on the solo SS-100 shook that viewpoint, and at the end of a two-day trial it required very careful consideration to imagine any little point where the side-valver scored as a roadster. The SS-100 is a racing machine only in its performance. The very fact that it holds the road like the proverbial postage stamp at all speeds is responsible for its behaviour at normal speeds—or what seem to be normal speeds—inspiring a high degree of confidence in the rider.

There is undoubtedly a very close connection between road adhesion and skidding, and, because the layout of the new Brough Superior has been planned with the primary aim of keeping both wheels firmly on the road all the time, the stability of the machine on a slippery surface is remarkable. For instance, in the failing light of a December afternoon the writer clumsily caused the front wheel to slip sideways off a projecting man-hole cover in conditions which nine times out of ten would have provoked a serious skid. In the present instance, although the pace was higher than it ought to have been, absolutely nothing untoward happened, and he felt inclined to go back and try the experiment again.

95 m.p.h. With Hands Off.

Unfortunately, there were no dry roads to be found during the test, else it would be possible to write of 95-100 m.p.h. at first hand. The machine was willing—in fact, simply begging—to be opened out, but the rider could not quite screw up his courage to do his part. However, the Brough Superior head tester had no qualms, and not only did he cover a gently curving quarter-mile on full-throttle—attaining probably 95 m.p.h.—but he removed both hands from the handle-bars at that speed for the benefit of *The Motor Cycle* photographer. The picture in the heading is of a second attempt, purposely slower so as not to elude the camera.

There is one other rather important feature about the steering. At speeds above 20 m.p.h. the front wheel centres itself and stays centred; balance and steering are automatic; and it would probably be extremely difficult

SPECIFICATION.

ENGINE: 85·5 × 85 mm. (980 c.c.) overhead valve V-twin.

LUBRICATION: Mechanical pump.

GEAR BOX; Three-speed with clutch and kick-starter.

CARBURETTER: Wex single lever (or to order).

TYRES: 28 × 2½ in. (or 3 in. to order).

PRICE: £170, Solo, £200, with Sidecar.

1925 Models on the Road.—

to provoke a wobble deliberately. At speeds below 20 m.p.h. it is not possible to steer hands off, and the rider must exercise a greater degree of conscious balancing than on, say, the Webb-equipped SS-80. With a sidecar attached, this self-centring steering becomes much more noticeable, and some people may not like it—at least until they become used to it. But it is obviously impossible to have things all ways, and the peculiarity of the SS-100 is at the right end of its speed range. The family sidecarist is not likely to purchase one.

There is no need to talk of such qualities as acceleration and hill-climbing—an engine developing at least 45 h.p. must obviously perform in an outstanding fashion in tests of that nature—but what impressed one most of all was the delightfully even pulling and the absence of snatch at slow speeds, and the efficiency of the brakes. To look at, the front brake is too small, and probably it will be too small for the machine of the distant future with its front frame and forks specially redesigned and strengthened like the modern big Continental car to take the major strain of pulling up; but it is much more efficient than one would expect, and, used in conjunction with the rear brake, it ensures deceleration being as rapid as one could desire and a good deal more rapid than one would expect to be safe on slippery roads. The long front lever comes conveniently to the hand, and allows the throttle to be manipulated simultaneously if desired. The rear pedal, of course, is similarly right at heel. What is the actual effect of the ribbed heat distributors on both drums it is not possible to gauge, but certainly unfinned brakes get extremely hot on occasion.

Neat Petrol Not Recommended.

Since standard compression is about 6 to 1, fifty-fifty mixture was used, and is recommended exclusively; but even so the pulling power of the engine at low speeds is surprising. Gear ratios are more or less a matter for the individual buyer, but anything lower than $3\frac{1}{2}$ to 1 top and 8 to 1 low would for solo use be absurd.

There is also an option in the choice of carburetters, but it is hard to imagine an instrument that would better combine a slow tick-over in neutral, a moderate fuel consumption at touring speeds, and a good all-out performance, than the Wex fitted to the test machine. Oil consumption, by the way, is phenomenally low, a microscopic setting of the pump being made possible by the cooler running of the engine and its, apparently, better oil retention arrangements compared with last year's J.A.P. twins.

Demonstrating controllability at low speeds

The Problem of Easy Starting.

Starting is an ever-present problem on a big twin, and the more efficient the design the greater the problem becomes. On the test SS-100 a quick and easy start could be effected by ignoring the exhaust lifter and simply bouncing the engine over compression, but this is a method which is only certain, when carburation, ignition, and general tune are "just so." Therefore, it is probably justifiable to criticise a fault which may possibly reveal itself after 2,000 miles' use without attention or after a careless overhaul. Sooner or later a substitute must be found for $3\frac{1}{2}$ to 1 geared kick-starters which may not turn the engine more than a revolution per effective stroke.

Another long overdue improvement which is not to be found on this, the most expensive machine on the market, is accessible hand-operated adjusting nuts for both brakes.

For the rest, it is hard to give anything but praise. The writer knows the little points of last year's SS-80 which were in greater or less degree unsatisfactory, and he recognises that all of them have received attention. Bigger brakes, roller-bearing hubs and steering head, a stronger gear box, and the provision of a transmission shock absorber in the rear hub, are improvements which cannot show their worth in a short road trial, but there can be no doubt of their ultimate value.

Of course, the 28in. wheels and $2\frac{1}{4}$in. tyres (3in. only if specially ordered), mark a change which may have a big bearing on the road-holding of the machine, or, on the other hand, may only serve to bring the specification into line with the machine upon which Le Vack did 123 m.p.h.

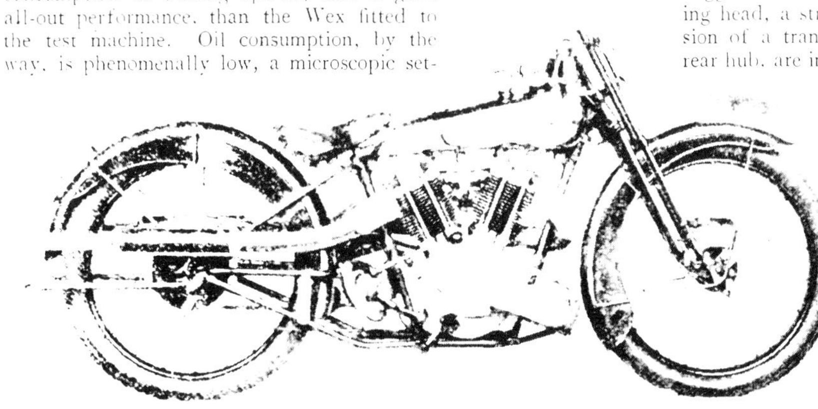

Very striking lines characterise the new model.

MOTOR CYCLE 3 OCTOBER 1963

208: TO GEORGE BROUGH

5. 3. 32 *Hythe, Southampton*

Dear Mr. Brough, It is the silkiest thing I have ever ridden: partly because of the perfect tune, partly from the high gear: but mostly because of the spring sprocket, I suppose. The gear is not too high. I can get down to 16 m.p.h.: and she pulls fairly at 30 m.p.h. and at 50 she is a dream. Just popples along so mildly that I can count the revs.

It was very cold but a beautiful ride. The back plug lasted till I got to Welwyn. The second plug is still running. I took two from your stores: so have made the cheque for 10/- extra, which I hope will cover them.

I think this is going to be a very excellent bike. The crowds that gape at her, just now, will stop looking after she gets dirty: and that may be soon, if only the R.A.F. give me spare time enough to use the poor thing.

I am very grateful to you and everybody for the care taken to make her perfect. Yours ever T E SHAW.

Lawrence's eloquent praise of his Brough is reproduced from the book "Letters of T. E. Lawrence." Below: David Dixon tries the famous flier

VERY superior

by DAVID DIXON

JUST what T. E. Shaw—Lawrence of Arabia—thought of his new SS100 is shown in the letter (pictured above) to George Brough in 1932. Lawrence has long since become a legend. So have Brough Superiors. He owned a succession of these big twins for, like so many before him and after, it was on a motor cycle that he had found his outlet.

So far as is known, only one ex-Lawrence Brough is on the road today—the SS100 mentioned in the letter to George. And credit for preserving that historic machine must go to a 27-year-old Portsmouth enthusiast, Les Perrin.

Just how well he has succeeded I found out when I had my first Brough ride the other weekend. Brought up in the mystique of the Brough cult, perhaps I was expecting too much. A strange beast? Yes, very odd and not to be judged on first impressions, for this mount is older than I and comparisons with contemporary machines would be unfair.

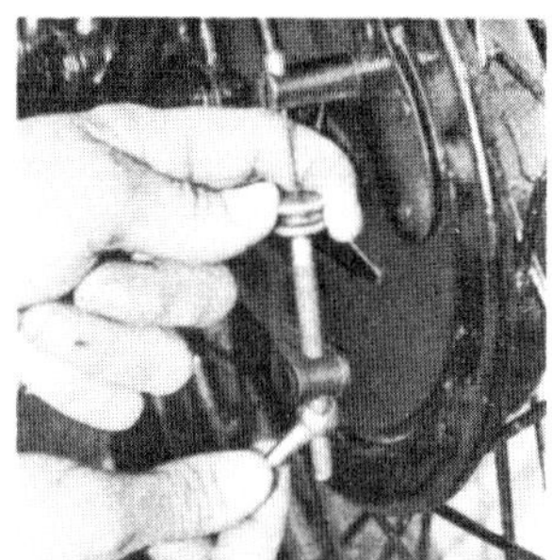

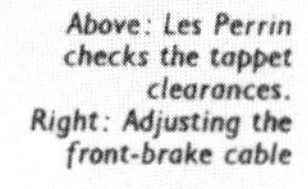
Above: Les Perrin checks the tappet clearances. Right: Adjusting the front-brake cable

MOTOR CYCLE 3 OCTOBER 1963

But where was the magnetism of these old vee-twins, the attraction that lured discerning men like Lawrence into owning a succession of such models? In the thirties, roads were uncluttered and the tempo of life considerably slower than now. So judge the machine in that light and it glows.

I had parked a six-fifty Triumph Bonneville and straddled the Brough. What a comparison!

WAFFLING

The old 998 cc twin seemed to come right from the horseless carriage age; lots of mechanical clatter from the exposed valve gear, a totally strange waffling burble from the exhaust and an impression of being astride a garden gate hinged in the middle.

Unkind criticism? Yes, of course it is, but those were my initial reactions. To gain a more lasting impression, I went off for a gallop across Portsdown Hill, overlooking Portsmouth. The Brough gathered itself together through the gears —oh, that awkward hand-change—and on a mere whiff of gas it settled into a loping 50 mph stride.

Only a mellow burble from the twin exhausts and some valve clatter were audible as I was wafted along on the breeze of yesteryear. The sheer effortlessness and cotton-wool punch of the power unit were something I had never known before.

I longed to tweak the grip just a shade sharper, but the engine had hardly emerged from its overhaul . . . .

Then a corner loomed up— no, the Brough is definitely *not* the world's best roadholder! The pivoted-fork rear suspension—a revolutionary feature 30 years ago—ironed out the shocks on the straight, but a long wheelbase and lack of hydraulic damping at front and rear made each corner a fresh will-I-or-won't-I challenge. I judge Lawrence had real fun on the swervery.

Leisurely motoring 30 years ago was hardly a testing time for brakes, and the Brough's anchors, even with new linings, were way down on present-day standards.

JUST RIGHT

Particularly pleasing was the comfortable riding position. Perrin had discarded the Triumph dual-seat which the previous owner had fitted and substituted an original Lycett saddle and pillion. To many of us a saddle may sound archaic but, in fact, it was most comfortable. Especially the riding position — compact and with just enough forward lean.

The traditional silver-finish petrol tank was missing —damaged in an accident, as was the original headlamp, but

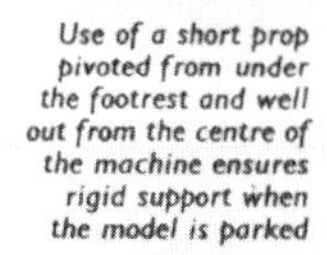
Use of a short prop pivoted from under the footrest and well out from the centre of the machine ensures rigid support when the model is parked

MOTOR CYCLE 3 OCTOBER 1963

Perrin hopes to find replacements soon. Also due for replacement later are the exhaust pipes; stainless-steel ones would match the twin silencers of the same material.

An Amal carburettor is the only other major item still short on the standard specification; it was replaced at some time by a Bowden. Otherwise, the spec is pretty well as original after two years of restoration by Perrin.

SURPRISE

Incidentally, as the original log book had been returned to a previous owner, Perrin did not know he had bought a Lawrence Brough—for £1! —as he towed the dilapidated heap away from a friend's garage. At that time a sidecar was fitted and only after discarding the old chair did he become curious and ask the registration authorities.

The Brough is powered by a 998 cc JAP vee-twin engine. The present Bowden carburettor is to be replaced by an Amal

Yes, GW 2275 had belonged to T. E. Shaw, of 14, Barton Street, London, SW1. Perhaps you didn't know that when Lawrence had finished in the desert he joined the Air Force, then the Tank Corps where he adopted the name of Shaw, and finally returned to the Air Force as an aircraftsman.

Of course, the knowledge that he had a Lawrence Brough, probably the only one in existence, spurred on Perrin's restoration. Major mechanical component was a new big-end assembly, price £6 6s, for the JAP engine. Various other minor bits and pieces were required and some items, such as phosphor-bronze bushes and valve guides were made by friends.

Some ingenuity was required, too. Gudgeon pins were not obtainable; Les found a pair of Vauxhall car pins which were the right diameter but ¼in short. So he welded on extensions!

More ingenuity went into the fabrication of a main-shaft bearing for the Sturmey-Archer gear box. But the gears and clutch, even the chains, were in good order.

The Lawrence SS100 today. Chief departure from original is the petrol tank; the hunt for a traditional silver-finish one is still on

Stripping and cleaning before painting produced most of the sweat and toil. Two tins of Valspar enamel gave a high-gloss finish.

And what did all this cost? A mere £19! But you must remember that some of the parts, which would normally have to be bought retail, were made by friends in the trade, keeping the cost low.

And those of you with insurance problems might care to know that the Brough was covered for £5 10s. by the DA scheme. Incidentally, the model passed its MoT test first time.

As those who saw the Brough Superior Rally last month realize, there are plenty of old Broughs lovingly restored and well cared for roaming the roads.

But can any lick Perrin's for distinction?

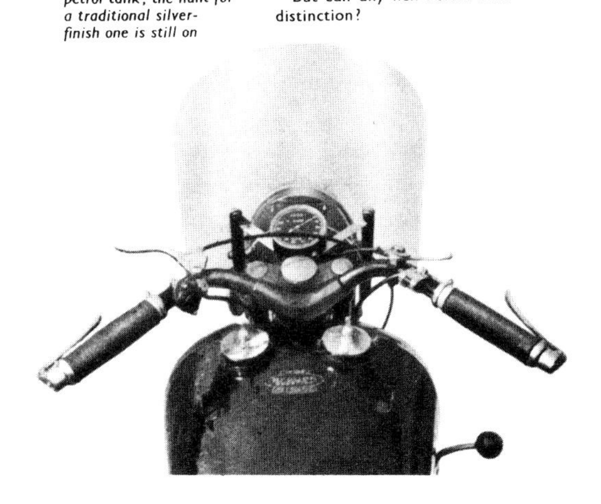

MOTOR CYCLING SPORTS MODEL ROAD TESTS

The Brough Superior, despite its massive proportions, proved most comfortable to ride, the position being definitely of the "armchair comfort" variety. Over rough going the rear springing proved a real boon.

The 999 c.c. Twin o.h.v.
Model SS 100
1938

BROUGH SUPERIOR

A Luxury Machine With an Out-of-the-ordinary Performance Permitting High-speed Touring in Comfort

WHENEVER a Brough Superior SS 100 is mentioned, almost the first question one hears is, "How does it go?" The name has always been associated with fast and luxurious motorcycling, and, at the conclusion of a strenuous road test of the 1938 SS 100, complete with sprung rear wheel, our tester found it difficult to give the machine sufficient praise. All the qualities which go to make long-distance travelling on two wheels comfortable, safe and rapid are combined in this outstanding model.

The combination of a large, comfortable saddle and rear-wheel springing permitted rough roads to be traversed without any shock being transmitted to the rider, a gentle undulating motion was all that could be felt on all but the very worst roads, and even over outsize potholes there was no tendency for the model to pitch. A ride on the pillion seat was a revelation and probably did more to demonstrate the advantages of the sprung rear wheel than sitting in the rider's saddle. A very smooth action was given by the front forks, and the steering at all speeds was beyond reproach, even when travelling so slowly that pedestrians were overtaking one, there was no need to use a foot for balancing purposes. At the other end of the scale no particular skill was called for at speeds as high as 85 m.p.h. or 90 m.p.h., the feeling

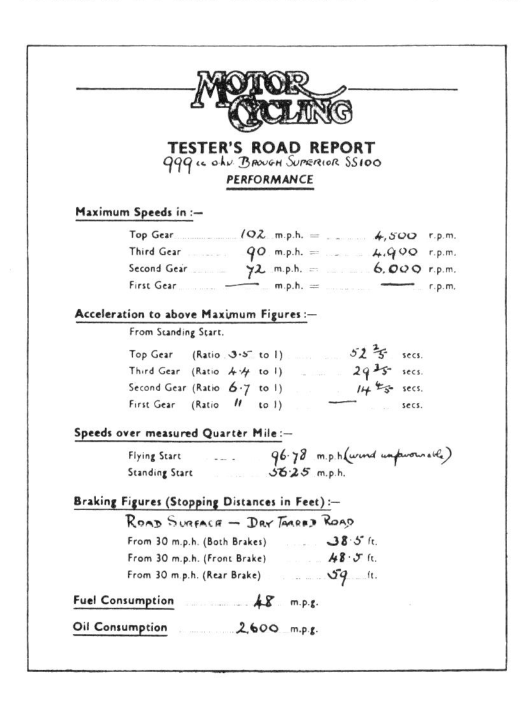

MOTOR CYCLING

TESTER'S ROAD REPORT
999 cc o.h.v. Brough Superior SS100
PERFORMANCE

Maximum Speeds in :—

Top Gear	102 m.p.h. =	4,500 r.p.m.
Third Gear	90 m.p.h. =	4,900 r.p.m.
Second Gear	72 m.p.h. =	6,000 r.p.m.
First Gear	— m.p.h. =	— r.p.m.

Acceleration to above Maximum Figures :—
From Standing Start.

Top Gear	(Ratio 3·5 to 1)	52 2/5 secs.
Third Gear	(Ratio 4·4 to 1)	29 3/5 secs.
Second Gear	(Ratio 6·7 to 1)	14 4/5 secs.
First Gear	(Ratio 11 to 1)	— secs.

Speeds over measured Quarter Mile :—

Flying Start ... 96·78 m.p.h. (wind unfavourable)
Standing Start ... 56·25 m.p.h.

Braking Figures (Stopping Distances in Feet) :—

Road Surface — Dry Tarred Road

From 30 m.p.h. (Both Brakes)	38·5 ft.
From 30 m.p.h. (Front Brake)	48·5 ft.
From 30 m.p.h. (Rear Brake)	59 ft.

Fuel Consumption ... 48 m.p.g.

Oil Consumption ... 2,600 m.p.g.

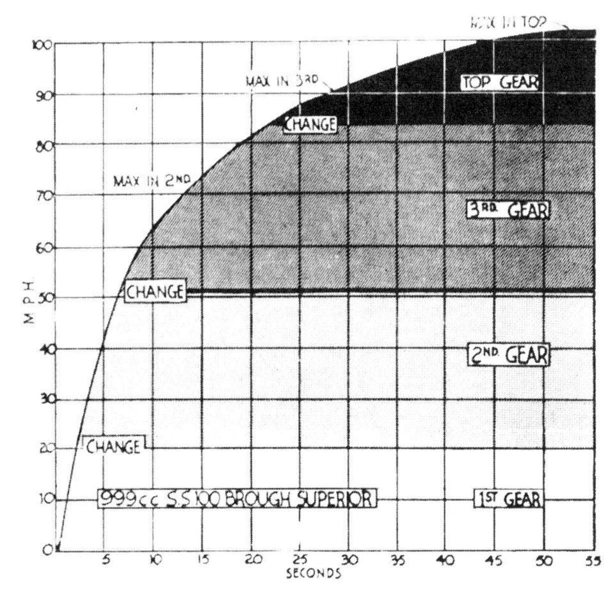

MOTOR CYCLING SPORTS MODEL ROAD TESTS

The SS 100, a machine to bring joy to the hearts of the big-twin enthusiasts and speedmen. The detail finish throughout is very fine and the equipment lavish. Note the Castle forks.

in parted being that one was travelling on rails.

Knowing that the weight of the model was somewhere round about 5 cwt., it was most impressive to find that the handling on corners and round fast bends closely resembled that of a good "five hundred." On many occasions when it was laid over at extreme angles round fast curves with indifferent surfaces, the handling was always exemplary. Factors contributing to this ease of handling were the riding position and the excellent layout of the controls, which were placed just right for a man of normal build.

The handlebars are remarkably clean; the clutch and the air lever being the only controls "clipped on," the front brake and the valve lifter are operated by inverted levers, whilst the throttle and ignition controls were both Amal twist grips, the control wires running inside the handlebars. The horn button and the dipping switch could be operated without moving the hands along the bars; the dipper being incorporated in the twist grip and actuated with a rotary motion.

Starting was always of a high standard, calling for very little effort. When cold, the best results were obtained by flooding the carburetter, about three-quarters closing the air and retarding the ignition a third; with the controls thus set the first or second kick (not using the valve lifter) was sufficient to bring the engine to life. When hot it was only necessary slightly to retard the ignition, and in nine cases out of ten the model would start at a gentle tick-over at the first kick, the twist grip being shut right back.

Great confidence was inspired by the brakes, which were smooth and progressive in action, although for really rapid stopping the front brake might have been more powerful. The advantages of a sprung rear wheel were appreciated when the rear wheel was locked on a rough surface without any sign of juddering.

An SS 100 enjoys the reputation of being one of the highest performance machines on the road, but possibly few realize the docility which a big twin can combine with ultra-high performance. For instance, a minimum non-snatch speed in top gear (3.5 : 1) of 12 miles an hour was coupled

The near-side layout of the engine-room showing the twin float carburetter, battery mounting and the forward-mounted Magdyno.

A close-up of the rear springing.

MOTOR CYCLING SPORTS MODEL ROAD TESTS

Not so big big-twin. The Brough Superior manages to retain a "classic" line even though it has a 1,000 c.c. engine. Interconnected silencers and cast aluminium fish-tails keep exhaust noise to a minimum.

with an all-out speed of over 90 miles per hour with the rider wearing touring equipment. With less bulky garments and " lying down to it " a maximum of 102 m.p.h. was obtained. Maximum speeds of 86 m.p.h. and 78 m.p.h. were obtained in third (4.4 to 1) and second (6.7 to 1) gears respectively; again, at the other end of the scale 11 m.p.h. and 9 m.p.h. represented the lowest speeds without any transmission snatch. Naturally the ignition had to be retarded when obtaining the low-speed figures.

The acceleration was little short of amazing. Reference to the speed chart will give a very clear idea of the figures which were obtained.

High Cruising Speed

So far as cruising speeds on main roads are concerned, the smoothness and general silky feeling of the machine as a whole gave very little indication as to whether one was travelling at 40, 50, 60 or even 75 m.p.h., the only speed at which there was a suspicion of a " period " was round about the seventy mark. This was not so much a vibration period as a phase of the valve gear, which made a slight clatter, thereby giving one an impression of roughness. Above and below this speed everything ran quite smoothly. As a result of this effortless speed it was possible to maintain very high averages over long distances with an absolute minimum of effort.

Taken over the whole test of about 500 miles, the fuel consumption worked out at a shade over 48 m.p.g. This included a considerable amount of town work and many miles on the open road. When purely engaged on a long-distance journey this figure improved to over 51 m.p.g., using where possible speeds up to 80 m.p.h. Oil consumption was also very moderate, only one pint being required after a distance of 325 miles, or, in other words, 2,600 m.p.g.

Very Quiet

As a whole, the degree of silence, both mechanical and exhaust, was of a very high order. The two large silencers and fishtails gave a very subdued yet powerful sounding exhaust note, which even when " flat out," never become at all obtrusive; in fact, several people (not motorcyclists) remarked on the silence of so large a machine. On the mechanical side the valve gear was commendably quiet, and this applied equally to the gearbox, with the exception of a faint whine on the indirect ratios.

Whilst on the subject of the gearbox, credit must be given to the foot change, which proved quick and positive.

At the conclusion of the test there was no trace of any oil leak either from the engine, gearbox or oil bath primary chaincase. There was, however, a certain amount of oil thrown off the rear chain due to the very adequate lubrication via the crankcase breather.

Roll-on Stand

Undoubtedly one of the essential features of a heavy machine is the ease with which it can be put on the stand, and in this respect the patent rolling stand takes full marks; it was only necessary to tread on a protruding lug incorporated in this fitment and give a gentle pull on the rear of the saddle to bring the machine on to an exceedingly robust central prop. The toolkit equipment was exceedingly good, and although no adjustments were called for during the time the SS 100 was in our hands, there appeared to be a tool provided for every necessity.

When correctly focused, the headlight was good, and enabled high averages to be maintained at night. As voltage control was fitted, no charging rates can be given, although it was noticed that with all the lights on, 30 m.p.h. in top was sufficient for the charge to balance the discharge.

Summing up, it is difficult to offer any criticism on such a machine. The finish is really superb, and the detail refinements are well carried out. In addition, the Brough Superior combines splendid performance and roadholding, and it is easy to understand why people who can afford to do so will pay £155 for a machine of this type.

BRIEF SPECIFICATION

Engine: 50-degree " V " twin o.h.v.; bore and stroke, 85.5 mm.; rigid crankshaft assembly with parallel-fitting shouldered crankpin, carried on oil-flooded bronze bearing on the timing side and three-row roller bearing on driving side; crankpin and mainshaft 1½ in. diameter; forked connecting-rod assembly with four-row roller big-end bearing; Lo-Ex alloy pistons with fully floating gudgeon pins in duralumin bushes; enclosed valve gear, hairpin valve springs; valves automatically lubricated; dry-sump lubrication; twin carburetters.

Transmission: Primary chain enclosed in oil-bath, foot-operated four-speed gearbox, ratios 3.5, 4.4, 6.7 and 11 to 1; final chain protected by guard.

Frame: Patented Brough Superior loop design fitted with patent rolling stand and fully sprung rear wheel; Castle forks.

Wheels: Fitted with Dunlop Fort tyres; front 26 in. by 3.50 in., rear 27 in by 4.00 in.

Tanks: Chromium-plated saddle tank, capacity 4 gallons; oil, three-quarter gallon.

Dimensions: Saddle height, 27 in.; ground clearance, 5 in.; wheelbase, 58 in.

Price: £155 complete with electric lighting, horn and 120 m.p.h. speedometer; pillion footrests, aluminium number plates.

Maker: George Brough, Hadyn Road, Nottingham.

OWNER'S VIEW

Owner's View

A doyen of the Brough Superior is Ronald H. Clark of Norfolk, author of the standard work on the marque, and an SS 100 rider in the past.

C.S. What of the SS 100, Ronald?

R.H.C. Impressions must be taken as a personal contribution with which others, perhaps, might not wholly agree!

C.S. You started with Brough Superior in 1930 (ohv 680) and have had an SS 80 since new in 1938. You must have seen many of the finest SS 100s. When did you first have one of your own?

R.H.C. I acquired my first SS 100, HOT 921, after the Second World War; a 1925 Pendine and identical to Cannonball Baker's 'Hop-along' powered by the unenclosed pushrod valve-gear JAP engine, with alloy coolers to each exhaust port and most neatly finned. The only modification was a Bowden carburettor fitted by some previous owner. Starting was relatively easy when this carburettor was not flooded, and with no flat spots at all during any sort of acceleration. The three speed Sturmey Archer gearbox could be operated by a hand-cum-foot lever, horizontal when in neutral. The Castle forks gave rock-steady steering up to 80 mph, the highest I, as a non-speed-merchant, managed to reach! But at that velocity the machine was still accelerating. One interesting feature was the ground clearance – a fraction less than four inches.

C.S. I've often heard you describe how trouble-free this machine was. What happened to it? I bet it's still going strong.

R.H.C. After a few year's pleasure I was persuaded to sell by, and to, a pestilential pesterer and in a short period, wished I had not!

C.S. But you weren't long without a '100, after that initial good experience?

R.H.C. It **had** to be replaced, and luckily I was able to purchase a rather more standard 1926 SS 100, now with enclosed rockers and pushrods. By a great coincidence it had been supplied new to a young man in the Waveney Valley (near Ronald's home) and registered PW 7680. It provided more effortless cruising up to what would have been the safe maximum of the moment. As with HOT 921, the alloy external ports kept the motor nicely cool. Road holding was again real Brough Superior at any speed. A goodly test of any machine is good steering at low as well as high speeds, and a photograph of my rounding the sharp left hander up Edge Hill's 1 in 4 on the 1953 Banbury Run testifies to this inherent stability of the Castle forks. It was this year, 1926, incidentally that the works first fitted a separate oil tank in place of a compartment in the petrol saddle tank. Again, some prevailer pressed me hard enough to part with it ... but yet another masterpiece came with me to dwell. This was no less than a September 1939 SS 100 with a Matchless BS/X ohv 1,000 engine with eight hairpin valve springs and a twin-float Amal carburettor!

C.S. This would be, from my experience, a much better stopper than the earlier ones. But what of starting and handling the rather heavier later model?

R.H.C. What about starting? To a somewhat elderly gent it was not too easy. But seeing a beefy youngster of twenty-two bring it into life second kick convinced me that any fault lay in me – not the quality machinery!

C.S. What about the performance and the ride? I recollect that this late '100 was as reliabie as the others had been once the valve gear was adjusted and lubrication was complete.

R.H.C. Twist the grip and 70 mph appeared rather rapidly to such an owner; 50 mph at a quarter throttle was the usual gallop on the level.

C.S. What about main road hills?

R.H.C. Twist the grip a bit and the summit arrived rather rapidly. Now it came to pass that with two Brough Superiors living with me, which deserved an easier life in approaching old age, GWB 985 went to a great friend on whose estate we all still meet on great occasions. With the proceeds, a stranger came from a foreign land and timidly abided with me to take over main-line and long-distance duties to the relief of the two Haydn Road pensioners. Oh yes, I still have two s.v. Brough Superiors.

Not quite the end of the story. One day from Sheffield I collected TO 7296, a 1925 classic Pendine with the three bands embracing the tank to secure it to the cross-plates on the cross bar, alloy exhaust ports, the lot. A heap of rust it was, the pannier boxes wet and sodden, tyres flat and so on. I aged rapidly, but started rebuilding. Later, I gave up, and a skilled craftsman in the village spoke unto me saying 'I do love the shape of that JAP valve chest cover'. Repeated quite often, it worked and knowing I could not complete it myself, I gave in. Two years later it appeared at my front gate, clothed in chrome, enamel, stoved, mechanically silent, mystic, wonderful. I see it often.

C.S. Did you test-ride it?

R.H.C. Only the foolish ask such questions! It had the most rapid acceleration, easily equal to that of the Matchless GWB 985.

Mechanically quieter perhaps was the Matchless, but examples from Tottenham always made you more aware of the hidden punch, when released.

To me there is nothing like a motorcycle powered by a big vee twin engine to cover the miles effortlessly. After a long or short period of time, depending upon the rider, one becomes aware of the 'charm of the big twin'. Difficult to describe but so very real, quite different to any other form of engine. A big vee twin pulling moderately slowly 'suggests a beat, akin to galloping horses' feet' and perhaps herein may be found the source of this subtle charm. At high speeds all had a roar of course, but never an annoying crackle or the carpet-tearing sounds of a modern two-stroke at 10,000 rpm. One could call it the song of the Brough Superior. **A deep low note!** To conclude with some famous words by Lawrence of Arabia in a letter to George Brough – 'The slow easy turnover of the big engine at speeds of fifty-odd give one a restful feeling'.

Very true!

For another and practical view I edited parts of taped conversations made years ago with the late P.J.C. Robinson of Westmorland, who at various times had 1935, 1925, 1928 (Alpine Grand Sports) models and often rode two of them during the same day. On one occasion, when I was trying to find an SS100 for myself in N.W. England, Peter asked me if I'd 'looked in every laithe barn in the North Riding first'. In those days, about fifteen years ago, SS100s were still being discovered under tarpaulins, under chicken guano, in greenhouses, in boxes in the attics, and I'm sure there are yet more so to be found. Not many, perhaps!

C.S. Your SS100s are a regular sight on Lakeland roads when you are at home from the sea. They are obviously practical touring machines, but what about steep bends, loose surfaces?

P.J.C.R. I do have a modern machine as well, but the 100s go as well. They are surprisingly light, very rigid, but the brakes fade and you have to be extra careful at watersplashes (fords) with the forward mounted magneto. They have given me great days.

C.S. What are the biggest snags with an SS 100, once you've found one?

P.J.C.R. There's a few. For example, there's a well known weakness of the Castle fork bottom links. The enamel should be carefully removed and the links examined for cracks; especially likely around the spindle and the pivot boss. Nickel-Sif bronze welds, stress-relieved, work; but peace of mind is rarely present for the aware, conscientious owner and new bottom links from a reputable source are the answer: forged items.

C.S. What other faults do you expect? I've heard that all the SS 100s are hard to start up.

P.J.C.R. Most owners neglect their magneto, and poor starting is very often due to no more than magneto neglect.

C.S. Special tips, not in the Instruction Book, perhaps?

P.J.C.R. Before starting, oil the pushrod ends, the rocker ball races and the inlet valve stems, and do not take it for granted that there's already H.M.P. grease in the pushrod end rollers and the engine oil is warm on a cold day! (It was from him that I learned to use diesel lubricating oil, very detergent, on all my clean engines, and with no complaints). Turn on the oil at the oil tank, switch on the petrol and lightly flood the carburettor. Then give a few gentle swings to get over compression, and the smart full-weight swing, as George Brough said. Remember to give oil by the hand feed oil pump when the engine is working hard. The JAP engine needs plenty of oil, especially the long-stroke motors. Oil consumption in a motor in good condition will exceed 1000 miles per pint but it is often nearer 500.

C.S. Rebuilding these engines is straightforward. There is the *Book of the JAP* by Pitman Books, and I found to my surprise a set of valve-springs for my 1096cc side valve in a cycle dealer's in Northallerton recently ...

P.J.C.R. Bearings and springs are one thing, but pistons are another! No-one should take on such a rebuild lightly; only when all the parts are available and the mechanic has sufficient experience and knowledge. The Pitman book is not the last word and there is no last word for the JAP range of engines, even those fitted to Broughs. But club membership is a great help, of course.

C.S. Would you agree that there are still some Broughs in the club, and a few outside, which are essentially in 'original' condition even of finish (with the patina of use, of course, and the blemishes to be expected) and that these are the most eloquent Broughs, such that new owners shouldn't automatically and entirely 'restore' them to 'as-new' (or better than as-new).

P.J.C.R. I know this is a bee in your bonnet! But I agree. However, it is necessary to regularly check spokes and sprockets when you adjust the chain, and lubricate all nipples and exposed metal. Not that there is much, on a Brough. There's something to be said for using cellulose paint. It chips, but it is easy to touch up, it seems better lasting than even some modern synthetics and don't Rolls Royce still use it? It has a certain look of quality to it.

C.S. The welded-up handlebar of the usual Brough Superior can be a problem if it has corroded within. (They used cables **inside** the handlebar, for neatness).
P.J.C.R. Yes, but the sound welded-up handlebar gives you a very secure feeling! And it imposes on you the idea, peculiar to Broughs, that you have to adapt yourself to the machine. That handlebar was to suit the original owner. Any quality machine imposes its own **character**. It isn't to be hacked-about.
C.S. Yes, but there's a tendency to fit, for example, Roadholder forks, Norton brakes ...
P.J.C.R. Too many, not originally specified for sidecar work, have had bent frames and ruined boxes. All because of fitting heavy 'chairs'.

BUYING

All genuine Brough Superiors are at least forty, and many of them over fifty and approaching sixty years old. Buying a well maintained example is, as ever, the answer; which practically means buying one with a good 'history'. **Caveat emptor.** Those with many owners over a comparatively short time may be expected, as with any vehicle, to be suspect. High mileage machines have many major replacements. This also means that nearly all have modifications and a previous owner's taste or requirement may not prove to be your own. The small number of machines, the much smaller number changing hands (even in the Club), speculation by 'collectors', dishonest description and inference, add up to a mountain to be climbed. Odd appearances of the marque at auctions – they are more rarely advertised in the motorcycling press than they were say 20 years ago – represent risk more often than opportunity. Commissions asked on sales, of buyers and of sellers, by some of the 'trade' must be remembered. A few key items *must* be examined first, and don't get carried away!

The crowning glory of the marque is set off by the bulbous but not bulky, gracefully lined but not meanly-limited tank (for the Brough Superior is thirsty, though the SS 100 is not notably so, even today, for its performance and age). Dents abound! The petrol tanks are basically of two patterns; the early narrow ones and the later larger-capacity wide ones which do seem to leak more readily. Soldered-up from many pieces, all curved, the petrol tank is the nightmare of practical Broughing today and there is no alternative but to find and pay for a specialist and sympathetic sheet-metal worker's service at the first sign of trouble. The rigid frame 1930s SS 100 uses the same oil tank as the 11/50. I have had several of these tanks, never a leak, but no two are exactly the same, as you'd expect of hand-made items individually fitted to different frames. We may not have the factory fitter's facility of choosing one to fit from the Brough Superior stores, but these are relatively easy items to come by and swap around amongst enthusiasts. So an untidy one may not put off the prospective buyer. But let him beware glass-fibre mudguards masquerading as the originals, paint over rusty chrome on tanks, and frames bent or broken inconspicuously. The works frame builder, and the builder and repairer of many tanks, have only fairly recently died, and such skills survive amongst a few experienced owners. Replacements and spares are likely to be available **eventually**, and all prospective owners should be prepared to support the Club's spares scheme, after joining, substantially; in the interests of all owners. The outlay only starts with the purchase price, and for much to be achieved by way of barter, the bases for barter must be bought; usually, after keeping the eyes open!

Beware of bikes in boxes! Brought as highly sought-after and some sellers are unscrupulous or just plain ignorant!! Broughs are still being turned up in unlikely places, but the most likely way to obtain one is through advertisement in the motorcycling press and especially through the club newsletter, which of course caters only for purchases by members.

CLUBS, SPECIALISTS & BOOKS

Clubs

The Brough Superior Club, now celebrating its silver jubilee, 'is operated in the interests of past and present owners of W.E.Brough and Brough Superior machines, to foster the preservation and use of the machines', but membership is not restricted to owners or former owners. Rallies, technical advice, the *Newsletter,* a spares service and a library are amongst the facilities available to members, who at present number a few hundred, many of long and honourable standing.

The club secretary, at the time of writing, is:

Peter Rhodes
15, Barnfield Road,
Ballington Cross,
Macclesfield, Cheshire

Membership is by application, with a stamped addressed envelope, and applications are published in the *Newsletter.* The Club needs BS enthusiasts prepared to work and enjoy the marque, not merely to treat the machine as investments!

There are members in many countries, and yet not thickly spread enough to form regional groups.

My impression of the Club is more that of an extended friendly family than the intensely organised and sub-divided 'organisation'. The marque is in devoted hands.

Books

Brough Superior – The Rolls Royce of Motorcycles by R.H.Clark. Goose & Sons, Norwich 1964, 2nd Edn 1974. (out of print)
This, the first marque history for a British motorcycle and itself already proved a limited edition in great demand, is the fundamental and worthy standard work. George Brough's foreword stamps his approval and many well-known owners, known to the author, are amongst the experts consulted.

All the models are dealt with, even the motorcars, and the SS 100 is set in its context of the sporting world and the development of motorcycling, with racing records in full, tables of specifications and engine characteristics, and pages from the manufacturer's Instruction Books.

Maintaining your Brough Superior
By W.S.Gibbard

It is notoriously difficult to write a readable, easily usable, technical book. The Author's apprenticeship must have been the hundreds of letters he wrote in reply to technical enquiries from any Brough owners and enthusiasts over many years, his letters being a model of clarity and "pitching". Bill Gibbard was technical adviser to the Brough Superior Club and developed a sixth sense when replying to such enquiries in knowing how much advice to give and what level of technical knowledge was to be expected.

Unusually, no publisher's name is given and no ISBN number.

Vital for building up a Brough Superior from bits, the book might be compared with Jeff Clew's very useful work on vintage motorcycle restoration. *The Restoration of Vintage and Thoroughbred Motorcycles (Haynes/Foulis).* Used with the R.H.Clark book, and with the detailed drawings which are found throughout the *Newsletter,* the book has enhanced practical value. It is not a workshop manual, but a guide and a vital part of the equipment to bring to bear on Broughs.

The Brough Superior Club *Newsletters* (the Club was formed in 1958) are, of course, another great and vital source of information.

The Club has also re-issued some Instruction Books and facsimile catalogues; very good value. The number of articles, series of articles, notes, letters and references to the Brough Superior SS 100 in the motorcycling literature since 1924 is legion, as I have come to know, and so also are the references to its rider/manufacturer, the inimitable George Brough, 1890-1970.

PHOTO GALLERY

1

1. Nearside view of the lean and handsome SS100. Note the low riding position, the handlebars where the hands would drop naturally forward, the back-rest on the carrier, rear stand and front stand for wheel service, and the evident accessibility of most other parts.

2

3

2. Offside view of the '100. The tank appears rather small for the performance of the machine, and the brakes likewise. Otherwise, little can be criticised in the appearance and in the practicality of such a machine. The magneto appears vulnerable, forward of the engine and low-slung, but it is shielded not only by its own polished alloy cover but also by the deep valances of the very efficient front mudguard. Efficient front mudguards are a great rarity nowadays!

3. Note the unobtrusive strength of the forks, their clean styling, the single rod of the mudguard support, the solid alloy embossed number plate and the lines of the mudguard.

4

5

6

7

4. Top of the fork tubes revealing the long compression-springs and the simple but secure brackets for the 'Lucas' acetylene headlamp. The manufacturer's logo can just be seen on the headstock, and again across the top of the mudguard.

5. Dignified balance in all components, with no wasted inches, for example, under the tank.

6. A study in line and gleam! The high finish of all parts, but yet not a flashy or over-fussy one.

7. Note the brazed-up handlebar bend, stronger and neater than an adjustable bar, and the milled alloy steering damper knob bearing on a large star friction washer. Personally, I find the knob too small, but it is hardly ever used.

8

8. *Rider's view: the uncluttered handlebar with spaced controls, long grips, twin filler caps and knee grips all adding to the symmetry.*

9. *Left-hand exercises; clutch, valve-lifter, and ignition levers all within reach of the generous grip.*

10. *Right-hand exercises: twin controls for air and throttle (there is no twistgrip) and front brake lever. The rear brake is operated by a foot-pedal, also on the right.*

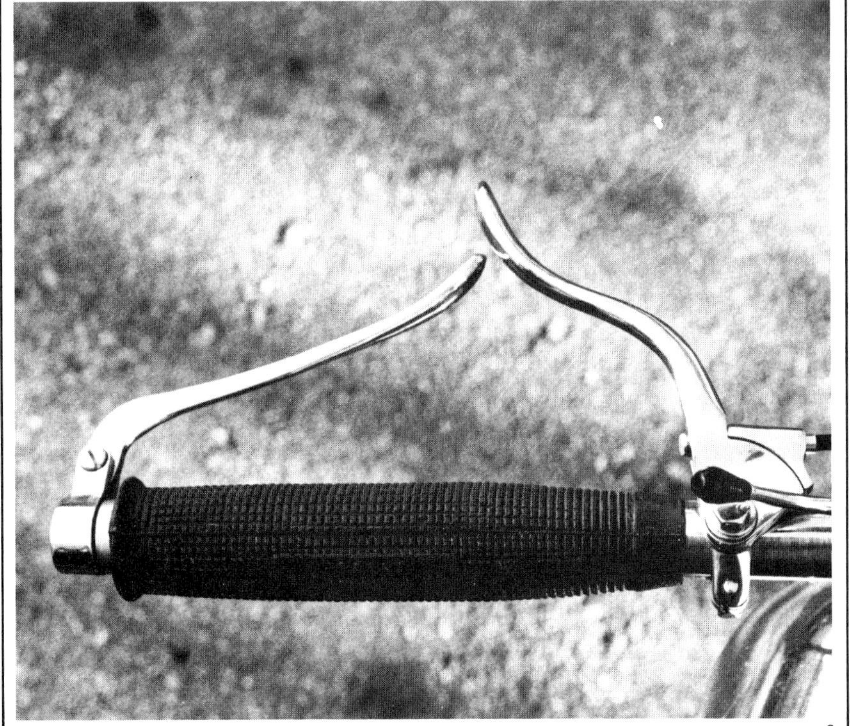

9

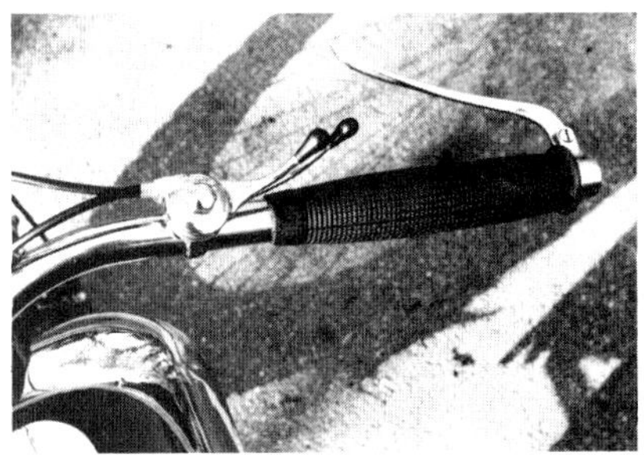

10

11. The tiny front brake, but see the assistance it has from torque arm, grease-nipples and star friction dampers!

12. Front brake from the nearside. A truly 'quickly-detachable' front wheel! Note grease points for fork pivots.

13. Rear brake. Note the thread adjuster to the rod, the neat rear axle adjustment. A better brake than the front!

14. The eye ranges over this assembly with pleasure! The high-level exhaust gets in the way of very little.

11

12

13

14

15

15. Not all Brough Superiors had hinged, and so secure, filler caps. But they all seem to have had the practical bar arrangement.

16. An accessible clutch. Note the drip feed to the primary chain, and the narrowness of the cradle frame itself.

17. Even the knee-grips carried the BS character!

16

17

18

18. The single carburettor, with remote float, incorporates a neat stoneguard. Clearly a simple matter to tune!

19

20

21

19. Note the accessibility of plug, pushrods, oil unions and magneto, under its cover!

20. Another view of the carburettor. The inlet manifold can be fiddly to fit free of leaks.

21. Note the elegant rear brake lever, the external oil pump, the acetylene reservoir and the built-up footrests evidently based on the Norton pattern.

22

23

22. On the left the simple John Bull plug-connector cover, and on the right the auxiliary (hand) oil pump.

23. The Best and Lloyd oil pump with unions and adjuster; the whole unit mounted on the crankcase and driven off the crankshaft.

24

25

24. *The JAP Tottenham on the crankcase.*

25. *A better view of the acetylene gas generator.*

26. *The cast alloy finned exhaust heat-disperser. Note the method of attachment of the exhaust pipe. Note also the sheathing of the control cables and wiring.*

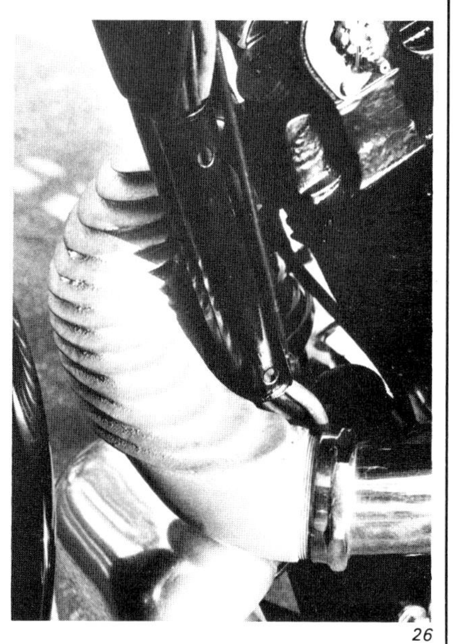

26

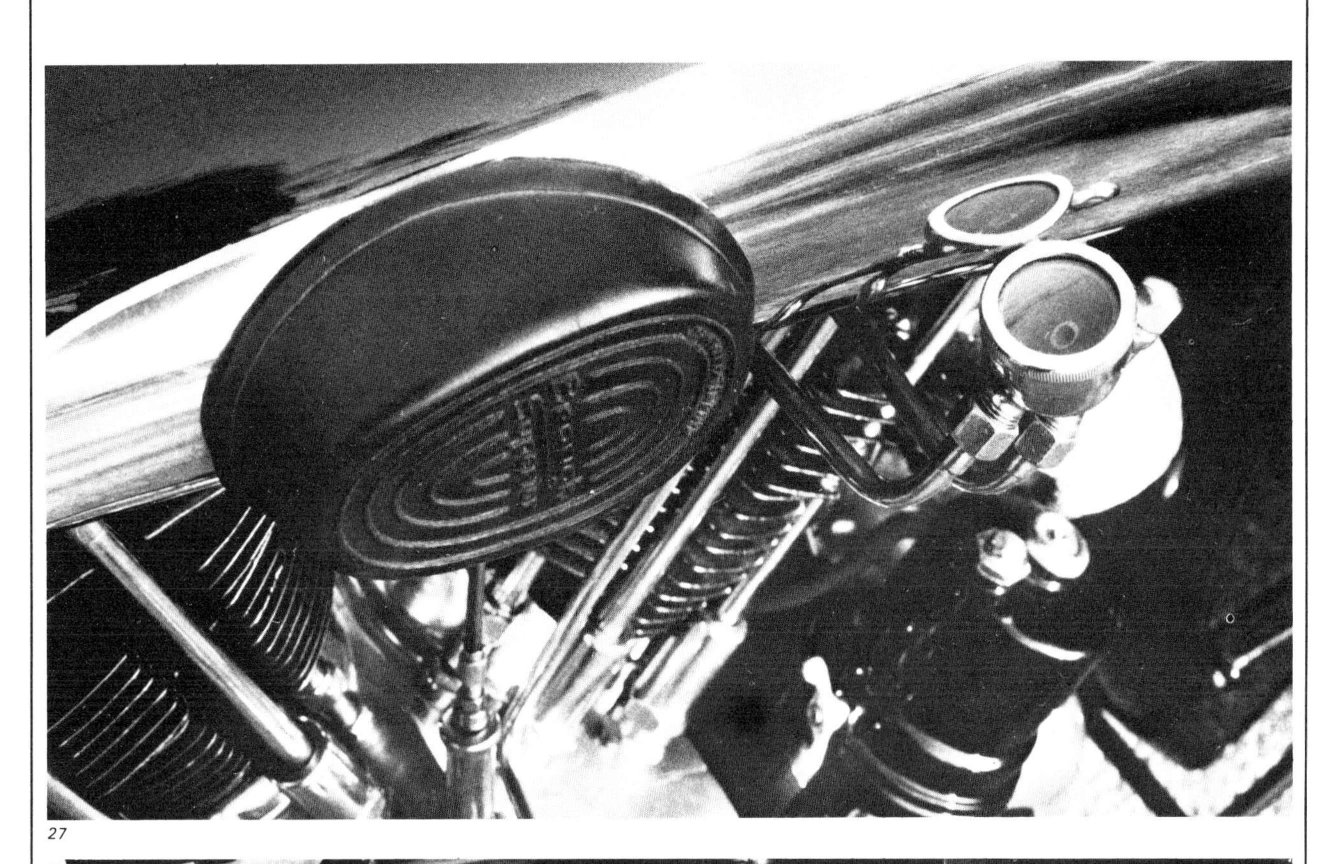

27

28

27. Sight-feed for the oil pump; very reassuring! The reflection shows the typical BS standard of finish.

28. The exposed JAP cylinder head components, with grease-nipples. The springs are, of course, on the nearside. Note the pushrod/rocker arm adjustments and exhaust system clips.

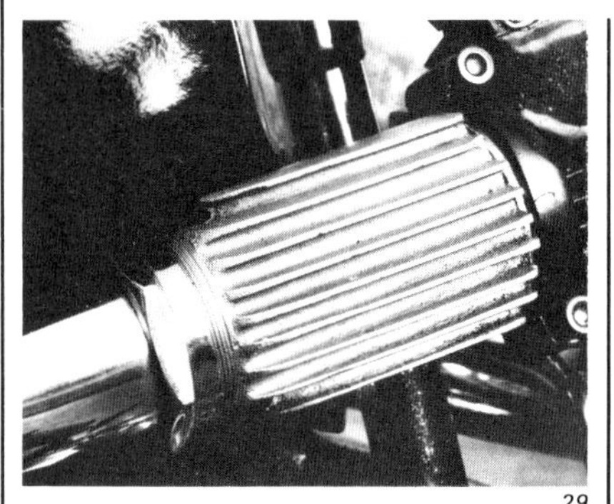

29

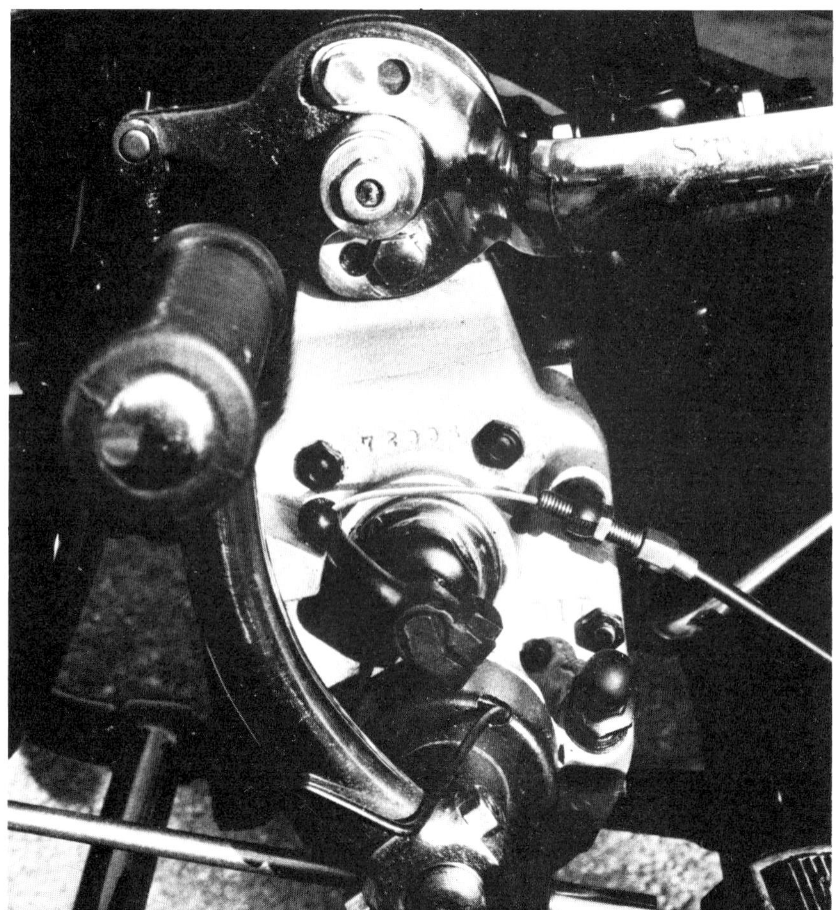

30

29. Cast-alloy finned exhaust cooler for the rear cylinder.

30. The heavyweight Sturmey-Archer gearbox, with selector-box and clutch operating lever above the kickstart boss. Again notice the narrowness of the cradle frame, and its construction.

31. Solid kickstart shaft and slender gearchange lever!

31

32. *The rear end; all compactness and convenience.*

33. *Nearside of the rear hub. Note the lightened chainwheel.*

34. *Again, a cast-alloy number plate. Note the tubular carrier with backrest and rear handle, the leather pannier cases in the steel shields, the finning of the rear brake drum and (on this example) no rear light. Otherwise, fully equipped for the tourist.*

35. *A generous pillion footrest (the rear carrier was good for occasional pillion use!) and the rear stand.*

36. *Why did G.B. have this logo at such an angle!*

32

33

34

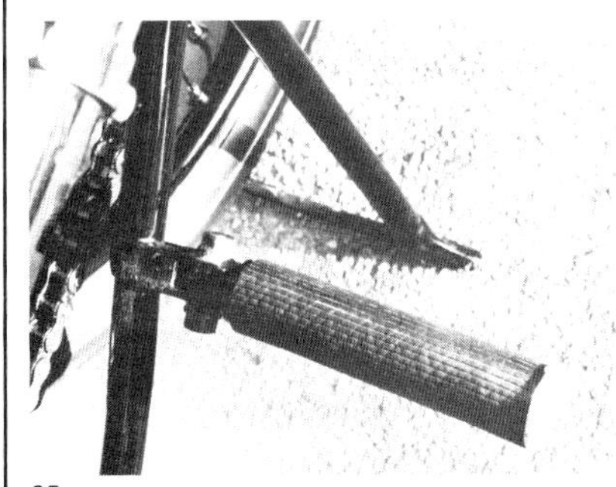
35

36

37

38

37. Nearside view of a specially equipped later 'SS100', with flyscreen, pillion pad, and other features specified by its original owner, T.E. Lawrence (of Arabia).

38. Offside view. T.E.L. usually had his service cane mounted along the parallel fork tubes, and a stainless tank.

39

40

39. *Note the slimness of the machine, overall!*

40. *The headlamp rim is not typical BS, but the general line and detail otherwise (note the 'Castle' fork) is!*

41. *Note the non-standard handlebar switch (right) and button (left). They clutter the original BS clarity. A few modern fitments are almost inevitable on any machine really and regularly used. The kink in the left-hand side of the handlebar is the only remaining evidence of the fatal accident.*

41

42. The gearchange arrangement, for the right hand, is a feature of this offside view. The foot pedal for the rear brake, is to the right of the alloy shield over the magdyno and is, as usual, embossed 'BS'.

43. Front end. The Castle Fork with the later design of mudguard stays, but still incorporating a front stand. The mudguards themselves are, as ever, deeply valanced and carry a cast-alloy embossed number plate. Note the larger brake of the later SS100s.

44. Brazed-up handlebar, clutch and valve lifter levers and horn button all to hand. But the wiring should be internal!

45. The battery appears vulnerable to road filth, even behind the mudguard valance. So also the horn!

42

43

44

45

46

47

48

46. The famous number-plate of the BS on which T.E. Lawrence died. A machine much treasured by its present owner. And no wonder!

47. Inside the right-hand filler cap the cylindrical filter holds T.E.L's spare petrol cash, sufficient in those days! These are the actual coins he carried.

48. Enclosure for the saddle springs, enabling them to be packed with grease. Another Brough Superiority, until the seals break down ...

49. Note the structure of the cross-bracing of the Castle Fork.

50. The later front wheel with improved braking and brake-torque reaction arrangement. A much improved, stiffer, function; but wear has to be watched for.

51. The beauty of the big JAP. Notice tap for oil-supply, under oil tank, full enclosure in an oilbath-chaincase of the primary transmission, and the rear swinging-fork pivoting both above and below.

49

50

51

52

53

52 and 53. Nearside and offside views of the upper pivot, damper and spring for the Bentley and Draper rear swinging fork. A neat improvement to road-holding, but needing careful supervision of bushes and wearing surfaces and regular checks for alignment.

54

55

56

54. The rear end, with solid sprocket, rear stand-spring, and an adequate size of brake drum.

55. The sight feed for the oil supply is now at the crankcase level, the pushrods enclosed in handsome covers mating well with the bold rocker covers. The magneto and dynamo, under their cover, are bevel-driven.

56 and 57. Notice the more generous finning of the later engine, the still exposed valve springs, and the hot air muff.

57

58

58. *The Sturmey Archer heavyweight gearbox is served by a remote, hand, selector box.*

59. *The Altette horn and the engine mainshaft shock absorber formed part of the specification requested by Lawrence at the time of ordering.*

59

60

60. *The battery is carried forward of the engine, in a somewhat unusual mounting bolted to the front engine plates. Note its quickly detachable fastening.*

C1

C2

C3

C1. A fully-equipped sporting tourer of 1925. The lighting, braking and comfort might be questioned by some today, but the SS100 was ever for a certain idealistic rider, and anyone who has ridden and got to know such a machine will see the efficiency and beauty.

C2, C3. The high exhaust system, less conspicuous than often in such systems today, with other lightened and tucked away features, emphasises that this is a direct development for long distance trials, and the product of a mind thinking of the practical, sporting rider, who nevertheless wants the best of everything. Notice the carrier, and the angle of the handlebars.

C4

C5

C6

C4. There is no spare metal here, no dead hand of the over-designer. Note the alloy cooling ribs clamped to the exhaust pipes, near the ports - very functional adornments. The forward-mounted chain-drive magneto may be considered vulnerable, despite the deep valance to the front mudguard and the polished alloy shield. Otherwise, this is a picture of accessibility.

C5. There is an old adage that you shouldn't be able to spit clean through, under the tank! Notice the sight feed for the oil pump, the alternative petrol tap positions, and the gold line between chrome and black enamel.

C6. Elegance both veteran (vide the lighting set) and vintage. And, one would offer, for all time. Notice the star friction dampers on the brake torque linkage, and the front wheel stand.

C7

C8

C9

C7. Notice the right-hand brake and gearchange. With the Sturmey Archer quadrant and lever, gearchanging can be effected by hand, foot or knee. Not that gearchanging is much needed. So many machines seem over-restored these days, neither as sent out from the works, nor as if used. This machine is an exception, somewhat above the original high standard of finish.

C8. The elegant Castle forks are well seen here; notice the springs in the forward fork legs and the milled alloy steering damper knob at the crown. Twin air and throttle levers, twin petrol filler caps. The auxiliary oil hand-pump can be seen to the right hand, next to the sight feed alongside the tank.

C9. Neat positioning for the acetylene reservoir, and typically JAP crankcase lines and plumbing. The Brough Superior logo was ever discreet and superior in style; hardly ever (except on some racers) blaring out loud. The lettering and initials are models of their kind, and unmistakable.

C10

C11

C12

C10. Further detail of the lower right-hand side, a splendid marriage of straight and curved components. The heavyweight Sturmey Archer box is not ashamed to show its clutch-operating adjustments, and most work on the clutch and gearbox could, of course, be done in situ.

C11. Uncluttered design speaking for itself, from before the days of twistgrip controls and long before the days of little lights and consoles! But George Brough was to pioneer twistgrip controls for lights, ignition and throttle. And hide many of the cables within the handlebar. Here, ignition and clutch are controlled by the left hand; air, throttle and front brake by the right hand. The handlebar is brazed up to fit the original owner.

C12. Notice the exhaust pipes alloy fin connection, and stoneguard carburetter protector. What pleasure such care in maintenance and use would have given the manufacturer.

C13. Left-hand view of the early SS100. See how exposed for attention, but also for dirt, both primary and secondary drives are. Note the grease nipples on the forks - not a machine to be neglected!

C13

C14

C15

C14. The lean lines of the 1932 SS100; lower, longer and narrower than so many other high performance machines. Black relieved by chrome (nickel, of course, on early machines) is a regular motorcycle understatement, but the air of purpose and balance, graceful and trim, is peculiarly Brough Superior.

C15 This right hand view is enhanced by the curved exhaust pipes and interconnected silencers, finished off by fishtail extensions. Harley-Davidson, for example, for some of the Sportsters, have effectively deployed a similar arrangement, but which modern manufacturer would have fitted such graceful and practical deep-valanced mudguards?

C16

C17

C16, C17. Left-hand view of the 1932 SS100 in its native habitat, an English country lane. Throughout their production, how low, beautiful, complete and comfortable they seemed and were. Notice how one component balances and complements another, as for example the bulbosities of the petrol tank, oil tank, primary chaincase and crankcase, seem even better in closer view. Note the Bentley and Draper swinging rear subframe, and how modern design begins to approximate to it.

C18

C18. Note the bevel-driven Magdyno with its handsome cover of polished alloy, the gate gearchange, fully enclosed pushrods and handsome, simple, rocker covers, the tall engine nestling neatly in the sturdy but unobtrusive frame, footrests and levers tucked well in.

C19

C20

C19. Further emphasising the compactness of the design and fitting, see how the tank and saddle continue and complete the basic lines of force smoothly, and match the Castle forks. Saddle suspension springs are neatly enclosed and the number plate is in solid alloy, numbered, rim embossed and highly polished. A machine with a long history wearing its pedigree.

C20. Note a few practical features; rear stand, easily removed rear mudgard section, stand and pillion grab, pillion footrest tucked away, easily cleaned and replaced exhaust system.